W9-AKE-250

Inventions and Discoveries

Architecture and Engineering

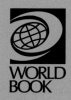

WORLD BOOK

a Scott Fetzer company

Chicago

www.worldbookonline.com

World Book, Inc.
233 N. Michigan Avenue
Chicago, IL 60601
U.S.A.

For information about other World Book publications, visit
our Web site at **http://www.worldbookonline.com** or
call **1-800-WORLDBK (967-5325).**
For information about sales to schools and libraries, call
1-800-975-3250 (United States), or **1-800-837-5365
(Canada).**

Editorial:
Editor in Chief: Paul A. Kobasa
Project Managers: Cassie Mayer, Michael Noren
Editor: Jake Bumgardner
Content Development: Odyssey Books
Writer: Rebecca McEwen
Researcher: Cheryl Graham
Manager, Contracts & Compliance
  (Rights & Permissions): Loranne K. Shields
Indexer: David Pofelski

Graphics and Design:
Associate Director: Sandra M. Dyrlund
Manager: Tom Evans
Coordinator, Design Development and Production:
  Brenda B. Tropinski
Senior Designer: Don Di Sante
Contributing Photographs Editor: Clover Morell
Senior Cartographer: John M. Rejba

Pre-Press and Manufacturing:
Director: Carma Fazio
Manufacturing Manager: Steven K. Hueppchen
Production/Technology Manager: Anne Fritzinger

Library of Congress Cataloging-in-Publication Data
Architecture and engineering.
    p. cm. -- (Inventions and discoveries)
  Includes index.
  Summary: "An exploration of the transformative impact of inventions and discoveries
in the fields of architecture and engineering. Features include fact boxes, sidebars,
biographies, and a timeline, glossary, list of recommended reading and Web sites, and
index"--Provided by publisher.
  ISBN 978-0-7166-0386-3
  1. Architecture and technology--Juvenile literature. 2. Architecture--Technological
innovations--Juvenile literature. I. World Book, Inc.
NA2543.T43A718 2009
720.1'05--dc22
                2008040644

Picture Acknowledgments:

Front Cover: © Ken Davies, Masterfile; Back Cover:
Lewis W. Hine, George Eastman House/Getty Images.

© Alamy Images 19, 29; © China Images/Alamy Images 8;
© Cosmo Condina, Alamy Images 20; © Gregory Davies,
Alamy Images 39; © Danita Delimont, Alamy Images 12;
© Digital Vision/Alamy Images 41; © Julius Fekete, Alamy
Images 21; © FogStock/Alamy Images 23; © Jereny Hoare,
Alamy Images 9; © Doug Houghron, Alamy Images 10;
© Images of Africa Photobank/Alamy Images 18; © Inter-
photo Pressebildagentur/Alamy Images 36; © Geri Lavrov,
Alamy Images 15; © William Manning, Alamy Images 25;
© Mary Evans Picture Library/Alamy Images 22; © The
Print Collector/Alamy Images 28, 30; © Scottish View-
point/Alamy Images 22; © Alexey Stiop, Alamy Images 43;
© H. Mark Weidman Photography/Alamy Images 11;
© Henry Westheim Photography/Alamy Images 27;
AP/Wide World 17; Bridgeman Art Library 4, 7, 12, 21, 31;
© Carrier Corporation 37; © Steve Chenn, Corbis 37;
© Hulton-Deutsch Collection/Corbis 24; © Gianni Dagli
Orti, Corbis 29; © Carmen Redondo, Corbis 11; © Vanni
Archive/Corbis 15, 34; © Franz Marc Frei, Getty Images 33;
© Time & Life Pictures/Getty Images 5; Granger Collection
31; Library of Congress 26, 40; © Martin Bond from Peter
Arnold, Inc. 42; NASA 16; © Shutterstock 6, 14, 19, 27, 44.

All maps and illustrations are the exclusive property of
World Book, Inc.

Inventions and Discoveries
Set ISBN: 978-0-7166-0380-1
Printed in China
1 2 3 4 5 12 11 10 09

▶ Table of Contents

There is a glossary of terms on pages 45-46. Terms defined in the glossary are in type **that looks like this** on their first appearance on any spread (two facing pages).

▶ Introduction

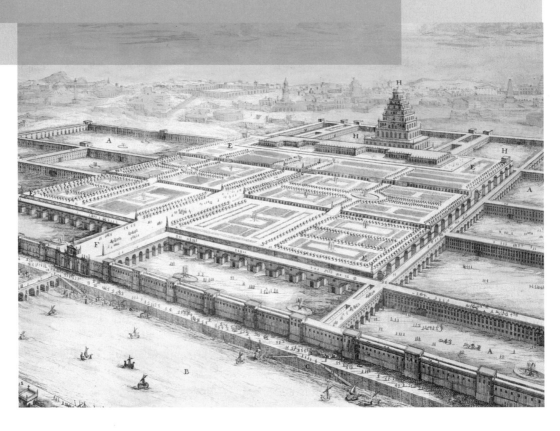

Ancient Babylon had some of the world's first great architecture.

What is an invention?

An invention is a new device, new product, or new way of doing something. Before the car was invented, people rode horses to travel long distances. Before the light bulb was invented, people used candles and similar sources of light to see at night. Today, inventions continue to change the way we live.

What is architecture and engineering?

Architecture is a term with different meanings, all related to buildings. It may refer to the art and science of creating buildings, practiced by artists called architects. Or, *architecture* may refer to the buildings themselves.

Engineering is needed in the planning, design, and supervision of the construction of buildings. It is also used to design such things as railroads, bridges, **dams,** machines, and electrical systems. These features are common to many cities and towns around the world.

Advances in architecture and engineering have changed the way we live. Millions of years ago, people probably slept in trees to avoid predators. In cold weather, they found warmth and shelter in caves. For many years, people moved from place to place, following the animals they hunted. As a result, any homes they made for themselves had to be small and simple enough to carry.

Eventually, advances in agriculture (farming) allowed people to stay in one place and grow their own food. They built homes that were more permanent. Over the next several thousand years, people started to gather together in the first early cities.

Over time, architects developed a wide range of new building techniques. They figured out how to make buildings strong and safe and how to

FUN FACT

Architect comes from the Greek word *arkhitekten* (*ar-kih-TEC-ten*) which means "master builder."

plan structures that served particular needs for communities.

As **civilizations** advanced, architects and engineers produced some of history's proudest achievements. Towering skyscrapers, historic monuments, and beautiful churches attract visitors to cities throughout the world. Today, architects and engineers continue to create structures that amaze and inspire the people who view them.

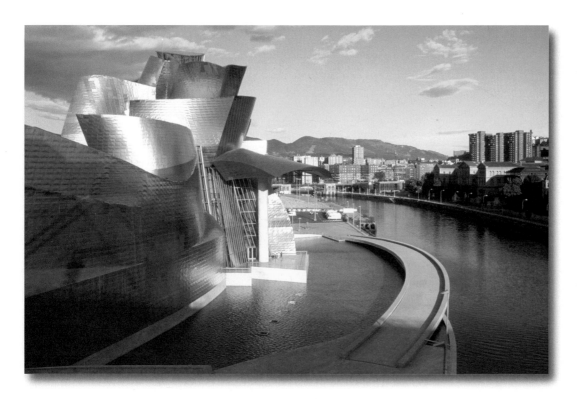

The Guggenheim Museum in Bilbao, Spain, resembles a ship sailing out to sea.

▶ Pyramids

In Africa, about 5,000 years ago, a powerful **civilization** grew out of the farmlands along the Nile River. The river made ancient Egypt a major center of trade. Over the next 3,000 years, the Egyptian people started to create amazing buildings that honored their pharaohs (kings).

The ancient Egyptians built marketplaces, temples, palaces, and other structures. However, they are best known for the **pyramids** they built about 4,500 years ago. Pyramids have square bases and triangular sides that come to a point at the top. In ancient Egypt, these structures served as tombs for the pharaohs and their queens.

Dozens of pyramids still stand in Egypt, but the three largest and best-preserved pyramids are found in the city of Giza (*GEE zuh*). Built between 2600 and 2500 B.C., the Giza pyramids were tremendous architectural achievements. The largest of the three, called the Great Pyramid, contains more than 2 million stone blocks, each weighing about 2.5 tons (2.3 metric tons). Some of the smooth stones that covered the

The Sphinx still stands guard before the Great Pyramid in Giza, Egypt.

Builders of the Egyptian pyramids set the heavy blocks on rollers and hauled them up ramps.

pyramid's surface have disappeared over time, but the pyramid itself has not shifted or collapsed. It perfectly keeps its original shape and design.

The builders of the pyramids faced great challenges. They had to move the heavy blocks to the site of each pyramid and then set the blocks in place. To make this possible, architects designed enormous earth and brick ramps around the outside edges of the pyramids. Workers then dragged the blocks over rollers, all the way up the ramps.

The Egyptian architects were talented mathematicians. Their measurements and calculations were so accurate that the Great Pyramid's base is almost exactly square.

The four sides differ from each other by a maximum of 8 inches (20 centimeters).

Just as builders today use rollers and ramps to move heavy objects, they also rely on exactly the same kinds of calculations the ancient Egyptians perfected.

The pyramids of Giza were built for kings about 2600 B.C.

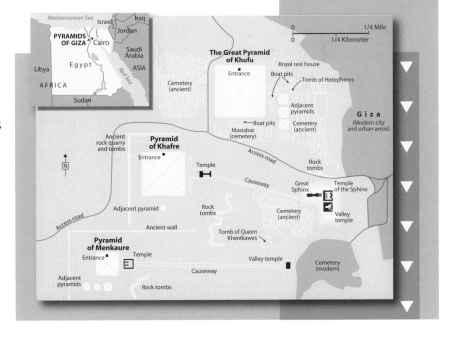

The Wooden Pagoda in Yingxian, China, is nearly 1,000 years old.

central government. Soon, great cities formed, and trade routes connected China to the rest of the world.

One of the most famous Chinese structures is a type of tower known as a **pagoda.** The first pagodas were actually built in India, where they were used as tombs. But as the **Buddhist** religion spread from India across China, so did the knowledge of how to build pagodas. Architects in China eventually perfected the style of the Chinese pagoda.

Pagodas are wide at the bottom and narrow at the top. They traditionally have 3 to 15 **stories.** Each story has an overhanging tile roof that curves upward at the edges. Most pagodas have eight sides and are richly decorated with ivory, bone, and stonework. They are often made of wood, though some may be built out of stone, iron, brick, or even gold. The ground level of a pagoda may house religious items or shrines. The upper levels offer views of the surrounding countryside.

Despite their delicate appearance, the Chinese pagodas have proven to

China has one of the oldest continuing **civilizations** in the world, with a written history that stretches back about 3,500 years. The area that is now China was once made up of many small states that relied heavily on farming. Then, in 221 B.C., a group of rulers conquered the states and formed a strong

be remarkably strong and sturdy. One of the oldest standing pagodas, the Pagoda of Chongyuesi Temple, was built about 1,500 years ago. Another famous pagoda, the Wooden Pagoda, was built about 1,000 years ago. It took almost 3,000 tons (2,721 metric tons) of timber to build it. The Wooden Pagoda has remained solid over the centuries even though it was built without a single piece of metal. Not even numerous earthquakes or wars have been able to topple it. It may lean slightly, but it still stands.

Chinese architects perfected the use of wooden posts and beams. Soon, their building skills influenced architectural styles in other parts of the world. Traditional Japanese architecture, for instance, is based on the same sort of construction with wooden beams and posts. This style produces structures that are strong and flexible—important qualities in lands that regularly experience earthquakes.

The Wooden Pagoda and the Pagoda of Chongyuesi Temple are just two examples of the many pagodas found in China.

Pagodas are often richly decorated, as seen on the roofs of the Heian Jinju Shrine in Kyoto, Japan.

FUN FACT Pagodas were traditionally made of wood and were much taller than any surrounding buildings. As a result, they were sometimes hit by lightning and often burned down after being struck.

► Cantilevers

The Firth of Forth Bridge in Scotland, built in 1890, is one of the finest examples of cantilever construction.

In addition to creating such structures as **pyramids** and **pagodas,** the architects in ancient **civilizations** also worked to build cities and to plan the roads that went through them. Among their contributions were some of the earliest examples of **cantilevers** (*KAN tuh LEE vuhrs*).

A cantilever is a horizontal projection, such as a balcony or a beam, that is supported only at one end. Cantilevers also support bridges. A cantilever bridge usually has two towers, or **piers,** at opposite ends. Each pier supports a section of the bridge, and the two bridge sections meet in the middle, where they are attached.

In Chinese pagodas, cantilevers jutted out from the walls to support the carved roofs. They also supported bridges that spanned deep canyons and wide rivers. Chinese architects used wood beams to build the piers of their cantilever bridges. They would crisscross the beams in such a way that the piers branched out in a wide Y shape at the top. At the other end of the bridge, the same steps were taken to build an identical pier.

Eventually, the two Y-shaped piers were close enough to one another that the road across the top met in the middle. This design formed a strong but flexible bridge. The crisscrossed layers left gaps through which floodwaters could pass without washing away the bridge.

In ancient Egypt, cantilevers were built out of stone. There are written records describing cantilever bridges that may have stretched over rivers several thousand years ago. Basic cantilevers were also used in the construction of military **fortresses.**

F U N   F A C T The ancient Chinese had an interesting way of building bridges over spans of water. To create a strong, stone **foundation** for the pier, they would drive piles, or stout poles, into the mud beneath the water. They would then place old boats between these piles, fill the boats with rocks, and sink them. They would stack rock-filled boats on top of each other until the rocks reached the surface of the water. Then, they would build strong piers on these rock foundations.

The Egyptians figured out how to build rooms at the top of fortress walls that jutted out over an open space below. These were used as lookout posts, and they looked much like the **turrets** that would appear on castles many years later.

The cantilever was a major breakthrough in **engineering.** Today, cantilevers are still used to build such structures as balconies and bridges. Many modern bridges use the same basic structure, only with different materials. Now, instead of stone and wood, cantilevers are built with reinforced concrete and steel. They may also be built with beams or other supports called **trusses.** (See Truss Support, pages 24-25.)

Cantilevers support the towers of Fort Qiatbay (above) in Alexandria, Egypt.

The architect Frank Lloyd Wright used cantilevered terraces in the design of this home.

► City Planning

Ephesus was an important city in ancient times. Today, its ruins (right) in Turkey are a popular tourist destination.

Mesopotamia was an ancient region in the Middle East where the world's earliest **civilization** developed. It was also home to the world's first architects and **engineers.** Between about 9000 and 5000 B.C., people established villages across Mesopotamia. About 3500 B.C., several villages in Mesopotamia grew into small cities. Each of these cities was home to several thousand people. In these areas, the earliest city planning took place.

City planning is the process of guiding the development of cities and towns. The planners in Mesopotamia sought to arrange cities that served the needs of communities. They set aside places where people could live, trade, worship, and govern. They built walls to keep out invaders. They also arranged for public buildings and

monuments to be grouped together in central locations.

City planning became more widespread as civilization advanced. Chinese cities started to grow around 2700 B.C., and cities formed in Africa after 1000 B.C. People were building cities in Central America as early as 700 B.C.

These cities were quite different from the early **Stone Age** villages. Many more people filled the new cities, and the people had different backgrounds and jobs. As cities grew in size and complexity, the need for good planning became essential. Planners had to think ahead and set aside central lands for public buildings and trade centers.

Greek and, later, **Roman** planners designed a number of beautiful cities. They brought in resources to meet citizens' basic needs, and they created public buildings that enriched people's daily lives.

Cities built during the **Middle Ages** (about the A.D. 400's through the 1400's) were not all that different from previous cities. Many still had walls around them, and central sections were devoted to trade, worship, and government. Often, the cities were built around an important central church. But as these cities grew, they began to face **overcrowding.**

This challenge continues to trouble city planners today.

Today, city planning is more important than ever. Cities that are not planned and maintained well can become dirty, run-down, or unsafe. City planners work to address these and other problems, and to guide the development of new city centers.

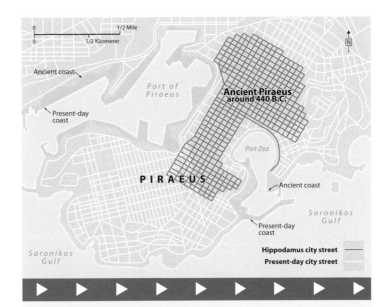

Hippodamus

Hippodamus (498 - 408 B.C.) was an architect in ancient Greece. He planned the layout of several Greek cities, including Miletus and Piraeus (see map above). He decided where buildings should go and created one of the first **grid** layouts for the cities' streets. A grid is an arrangement of intersecting vertical and horizontal lines. Today, the idea of laying out a city in a grid plan is called "Hippodamian," even though these sorts of layouts may have already been in use in other cities.

► Aqueducts

The Pont du Gard aqueduct, outside Nimes, France, was built by the Romans nearly 2,000 years ago.

One of the great challenges faced by early city planners involved water. In particular, how could a large city provide enough fresh water for all of its citizens? Even when cities were built along a river or other waterway, the water supply was often **polluted** with waste.

When ancient Rome was founded in 753 B.C., it was a small city set among seven hills. At its peak, in the A.D. 100's and 200's, the empire (group of nations) covered half of Europe, stretching as far north as Scotland and as far south as northern Africa. Rome also ruled much of the Middle East. Within this large territory were large cities filled with many thousands of people—all of whom needed clean water.

The **Romans** addressed this issue with the help of skills they learned from the people of Jerusalem, a city in the Middle East. In Jerusalem, architects had figured out how to make a basic **aqueduct** (*AK wuh duhkt*). An aqueduct is a stone channel through which water flows from one place to another. The Romans adopted the basic aqueduct structure and perfected it. By A.D. 97, nine aqueducts were carrying about 85 million gallons (322 million liters) of water daily into the city of Rome.

Rome shared this technology with the cities it ruled. Eventually, more than 200 Roman cities, spread throughout the empire, had aqueducts. A famous Roman aqueduct called the Pont du Gard still stands near Nimes, France.

After the Roman Empire split apart in A.D. 395, many cities still used the old aqueducts. Very few new ones were built until the **Middle Ages.** Eventually, late in the 1500's, Sir Francis Drake designed and built an aqueduct in the English town of Plymouth. In 1609, an aqueduct that was 38 miles (61 kilometers) long was constructed to carry fresh water into London.

Today, underground pipes carry water to most people who live in urban areas. Occasionally, though, communities still rely on aqueducts.

The Hetch Hetchy aqueduct in California supplies 2.5 million people with water.

Marcus Agrippa

Marcus Agrippa (63-12 B.C.) was a Roman general who worked closely with Augustus, the first emperor of Rome. Agrippa helped Augustus gain control of Rome during a time of civil war. He helped the emperor set up the Roman government, and he was the first person in history to be in charge of a city's waterworks. Many of Rome's aqueducts were built on his orders. Agrippa was supposed to become emperor after Augustus died, but he himself died before Augustus did.

▶ Dams

The Aswan High Dam, on the Nile River in southeastern Egypt, provides flood control, hydroelectric power, and water for farming.

Dams block water as it flows, causing it to form a **reservoir.** Once the reservoir reaches the desired size, the dam lets water flow out again, so that the stream can continue.

The earliest dams probably looked a lot like the dams that beavers build. They were most likely made of piled brush or logs, or even stone. These dams worked temporarily, but they could be washed away if the waters rose too high.

The Egyptians built the first known dam around 2800 B.C. Later, Romans built dams throughout their empire, constructing them out of perfectly cut stone blocks. Some of these dams still stand and are still in use today.

Over the centuries, people continued to build dams out of many different kinds of materials. The dams became stronger and safer, and people found new uses for them. In some areas, dams helped prevent damaging floods. Some people learned to use the flowing water at dams to grind grain. In modern times, the rapidly flowing water can be used to generate electric power for entire cities.

While the ancient **Romans** used **aqueducts** to carry water to citizens, people in other lands developed ways to control the water that they needed. If a community lacked water, farmers could not grow crops, and people could lose their food supply. This problem was especially serious in the hot, dry climates of the Middle East and northern Africa.

People had to figure out how to store water so that it would be available during the dry seasons, when small streams typically dried up. Eventually, they found that they could trap water by building **dams** across rivers.

Though many people benefit from dammed water, the construction of dams can harm the environment. When too much water is stored during a **drought,** rivers below the dam can dry out, causing plants and animals that depend on the rivers to die. Also, lands may be swallowed up as water rises to form the reservoir. Still, dams are a key method of controlling water for communities, and they continue to be built to this day.

When completed, the Three Gorges Dam in China will be able to power up to 34 cities.

A CLOSER LOOK

The world's largest dam, the Three Gorges Dam, spans the Yangtze River in China. Designed to control flooding and to generate electric power, the dam is about 1.3 miles (2.1 kilometers) long and 610 feet (186 meters) tall. Eventually, the reservoir behind it will stretch upstream nearly 400 miles (644 kilometers). Millions of people have had to move to new lands as the rising reservoir waters have approached their homes.

Arches

Architects have long sought to make buildings that reflect the pride of a community. As a result, many **civilizations** have become known for their particular architectural structures and designs. In ancient Rome, one of the key architectural features was the **arch.**

No one is exactly sure when people first figured out how to use the arch in construction. At the time the first arch was built, perhaps as early as 3500 B.C., people knew how to build flat roofs supported by walls or **columns.** Arches required a more complex building technique.

Traditionally, people built arches by arranging stone blocks. During construction, the blocks are supported with a wooden frame. The last block placed, the **keystone,** sits in the middle between the two sides of the arch. Each side of the arch presses against the keystone. This pressure keeps the arch up when the wooden frame is removed.

When an arch is properly built, it can support great weight. An arched

The Triumphal Arch at Volubilis, Morocco, was built for Roman Emperor Caracalla in A.D. 217.

The tallest monument in the United States is the Gateway Arch in St. Louis, Missouri. The giant arch, wrapped in stainless steel, rises 630 feet (192 meters) above downtown St. Louis, on the Mississippi River. The arch was built in the 1960's to honor the nation's westward expansion during the 1800's. Visitors can travel up the arch to a room that offers views of the city.

doorway, for instance, can support a heavy roof or additional **stories** built above it.

Although early architects figured out how to build an arch, the construction process required a great deal of work. As a result, they did not become a common part of architecture until the ancient **Romans** started using them to build **aqueducts** and bridges. Romans also used this technique to create arches that honored their leaders.

Roman architects soon developed new uses for the arch. They began using them inside buildings to create rooms with **vaulted** (arched) ceilings. With a vaulted ceiling, a Roman room no longer needed to use columns in the middle of the room as support structures. The ceiling could be supported only by the outer walls.

In the **Middle Ages,** people modified the arch design to build pointed arches. They also arranged the arches in rows to make long hallways called **arcades.**

Today, arches are built out of concrete or steel, in addition to the traditional stone. Yet, even with ancient techniques and primitive materials, many of the arches built thousands of years ago still stand.

The chapel of the Mosteiro dos Jerónimos in Portugal has a large, vaulted ceiling. The chapel was constructed in the A.D. 1500's.

▶ Domes

The opening in the dome of the Roman Pantheon floods the room with light.

As cities grew, architects looked for new ways to make important buildings look more grand. Over time, spectacular **domes** appeared atop a number of major buildings.

In **Buddhist** countries, people built bell-shaped structures called **stupas** that marked sacred places or honored special events. In ancient Rome, architects improved on **arch**-building technology and built an actual dome.

The Pantheon is a **Roman** temple that was completed about A.D. 126.

Its walls were constructed in a circle, and they support a rounded dome roof. Even though it is nearly 2,000 years old, the Pantheon is still considered one of the largest masonry (stone) domes ever built. It stands 142 feet (43 meters) tall and measures 142 feet (43 meters) across.

At the time the Pantheon was built, most architects focused on how a building appeared from the outside. With the Pantheon, however, the building's interior (inside) was especially magnificent. The Pantheon has an opening in the high center of the

The dome of the Hagia Sophia in Istanbul, Turkey, rests on arches and four sturdy piers.

dome, which allows natural light to flood the room. The building's brass doors, gleaming stonework, and works of art are showcased perfectly.

People have constructed numerous domes in the centuries since the Pantheon was designed. The Hagia Sophia, completed in Constantinople (now Istanbul, Turkey) in A.D. 537, is especially impressive. St. Peter's Basilica in Vatican City and the Cathedral of Florence in Italy are magnificent examples of domes built during the **Renaissance.**

Most **Muslim** mosques are built with dome-shaped roofs. Occasionally, countries use domes for important government buildings, such as the United States Capitol. Sometimes, architects design domes so massive they can cover sports stadiums. Some modern stadiums have domes that can be opened or closed.

Filippo Brunelleschi

Filippo Brunelleschi (1377?-1446) was an Italian architect who designed the dome of the Cathedral of Florence in Italy. He solved the problem of how to keep the walls of the cathedral from splaying outward and collapsing, which would naturally happen under the enormous weight of the dome. Rather than prop up the walls with massive structures called buttresses, he wrapped a large iron chain around the outside walls, which held them in place. Brunelleschi is also famous for a trick he played that helped him win the job of designing the cathedral. He challenged his competitors to stand an egg on its end on a smooth stone counter top. No one could do it. When it came to be his turn, he smashed the end of the egg, and it stood up easily.

▶ Drawbridges

As cities grew and new trade routes were established, people worked to make transportation easier. In particular, they designed bridges to allow people to cross over obstacles, such as rivers and canyons. Bridges made it easier for travelers to reach cities. However, there was a major drawback: the bridges also made travel easier for enemies and invaders.

To address this problem, people sought to develop bridges that could provide access for friendly travelers while at the same time keeping enemies away. During the **Middle Ages,** castle architects in Europe figured out a solution. They developed movable bridges, called **drawbridges,** that stretched over castle **moats.** When castle owners wanted to

Drawbridges help keep out enemies. The Caerlaverock Castle in Scotland (above) now has a pedestrian bridge where its drawbridge once stood.

The Burnside Bridge in Portland, Oregon, splits to allow ships to pass beneath.

cross the moat, they went over the bridge. Then, to keep out other people, they simply raised the bridge so that it could not be crossed. In addition, the raised bridge acted like a sturdy front door, solidly covering the main entrance to the castle.

Today, drawbridge technology is used to provide safe passage for tall boats that must pass underneath low bridges. When a drawbridge spans a waterway, it can be raised up, splitting in the middle, to allow boats to pass through. After the boat has passed, the bridge is lowered, allowing people to again cross the waterway.

There are three main kinds of movable bridges. Bascule bridges, or drawbridges, tilt up and open in the middle. Vertical-lift bridges have a section that rises up into the air.

This section stays flat, like the floor of an elevator, and breaks away from the road on both sides. Swing bridges do just what their name suggests. They swing to the side when a boat needs to pass and then swing back again after the boat has gone through.

FUN FACT

Castle moats were a good form of defense. They could be quite deep and filled with water, and they kept enemies from being able to rush at the castle walls. In addition, the moats often contained waste from the castle's residents. Today, many moats are dried out, and archaeologists dig in them to learn more about the people who lived in the castles long ago.

► Truss Support

While **drawbridges** showed a great leap forward in bridge design, architects did not stop there. Newer, more sophisticated bridges emerged in the 1500's. Around this time, people started to use their mastery of metal, stone, and wood to create completely new shapes that could cover much wider spans.

Many of the new bridges used **trusses.** Trusses are beams or other supports that are usually connected in a series of triangles. In this arrangement, small triangles are grouped together to form larger triangles.

The triangle is a strong shape for building. It can withstand great pressure pushing down on it, which makes it the ideal shape to carry the weight of a bridge. Even though the triangles may be built out of fairly thin beams, they are much stronger than the usual strength of the materials from which they are made.

Truss technology was not com-

The Royal Albert Bridge opened in 1859. It uses oval-shaped trusses to cross the River Tamar in England.

In Ontario, Canada, the trusses of the Royal Alexandria Bridge carry it over the Ottawa River.

pletely new in the 1500's. In fact, people in the Middle East had been using versions of the truss as far back as 2500 B.C. The ancient Greeks often built trusses into their roofs. But it wasn't until the development of the new bridges that **engineers** began to understand the true possibilities for trusses in construction.

Over time, people started building truss bridges over wider and wider spans. A modern truss bridge can have a span of more than 1,000 feet (305 meters). The majority of modern truss bridges have the roadway on top of the trusses and are called deck truss bridges. The roadway of a through truss bridge runs between the trusses.

Today, when engineers design new bridges, they have a variety of bridge-building technologies to choose from. In some cases, it is easi-

est to just use massive steel **girders** (beams) that lay across supports to create a road. Still, many engineers prefer to build truss bridges. Truss bridges are elegant and strong, and their construction requires fewer materials and less heavy equipment.

FUN FACT

The Inspired Carpenters were three early American carpenters who specialized in building truss bridges in the early 1800's. Timothy Palmer (1751-1821), Lewis Wernwag (1770-1843), and Theodore Burr (1771-1822) built truss bridges that allowed people to move into and settle the American wilderness. Palmer is believed to be the first builder to cover the truss bridge, which led to the trend of building covered bridges in many areas of the United States.

Suspension Bridges

The Niagara Falls Suspension Bridge opened in 1855. It allowed pedestrians, carriages, and trains to cross from Niagara Falls, New York, to Niagara Falls, Ontario.

The use of **trusses** brought great improvements to bridge design, but certain problems still remained. Truss bridges could only span wide distances if there were strong bases into which the **piers** could be anchored. The bridges could not be used in places where fast-moving water or extremely steep canyons made it impossible to build sturdy piers.

For centuries, people had used twisted vine or braided bamboo cables to create simple **suspension bridges.** They would hang the cables from supports on opposite sides of the bridge, and a path or roadway would hang below the cables. The hanging roadway somewhat resembled the seat on a swing.

By the early 1800's, people had improved on this basic design, and they began to construct massive suspension bridges. The roads on these bridges hung from iron chains rather than braided vines.

Over time, the builders of suspension bridges faced a number of challenges. Could they build a bridge that would stay stable and strong when pushed by high winds or battered by storms? Could the suspension cables support the great weight of the roadway, plus whatever vehicles were traveling over it? Could they build suspension bridges capable of withstanding earthquakes?

In the mid-1800's, an American **engineer** named John Augustus Roebling figured out the answers to many

The Golden Gate Bridge in San Francisco, California, was built between 1933 and 1937. It looks light and airy, but it contains 88,000 tons (79,832 metric tons) of steel and 390,000 cubic yards (356,616 cubic meters) of concrete. There are 160,000 miles (257,495 kilometers) of wire in just the two main cables. That's enough wire to wrap around Earth's equator six and a half times!

of these questions. He introduced a breakthrough in bridge design when he combined the strength of truss supports below the roadway with the strength of cables hanging from above. These combined to make a bridge so strong that it could cross over the rushing waters of Niagara Falls, on the border between New York and Ontario, Canada. Roebling used similar techniques for a bridge he built over the Ohio River in Cincinnati, Ohio, and the Brooklyn Bridge in New York City.

Today, suspension bridges are built to span great distances. One of the most famous suspension bridges is the Golden Gate Bridge, which spans 4,200 feet (1,280 meters) of open water in San Francisco.

In some countries, suspension bridges are built from bamboo and rope.

Builders of the Thames Tunnel in London, England, used a tunnelling shield to prevent the tunnel from collapsing while they worked.

As people invented forms of transportation that allowed them to travel faster and farther, they also turned their attention to improving roadways. Over the centuries, architects perfected the bridges they needed to cross rivers and canyons. Similarly, people searched for ways to build tunnels through other obstacles, such as mountains.

There are signs that people in Africa used deer antlers and horse bones to dig tunnels as far back as 10,000 years ago. Over the centuries, people developed better tools for digging and discovered ways to stay safe while underground. For example, they learned how to support the roof of the tunnel, so that the rocks and dirt would not collapse onto them. People who worked in **mines** were responsible for many early advances in tunnel design.

Tunnel building became faster and easier with the development of explosives. People could blast out large sections of rock and then use carts to carry away the rubble.

During the 1800's, railroad travel made tunnel building even more important. Trains could not safely travel up and down steep slopes, so they depended on tunnels and bridges to pass across mountains and valleys.

As people built more and more tunnels, they also figured out how to build through soft, shifting soil. In 1825, English workers created a **tunnelling shield** that allowed them to build a railroad tunnel under the River Thames, which runs through the middle of London. The shield was a cylinder that held up the material around the tunnel while workers constructed supports of iron, steel, and concrete. It took 18 years to build the

Ancient Egyptians were master tunnel builders. They created tunnels for many reasons: to store water in underground rooms, to mine precious metals, and to make hidden entrances to tombs. Though they had to chip away at the rock by hand, they also invented an efficient way to break the rock. They would build fires in front of the rock, and then pour water over the superheated surface. The water would flow into cracks in the rock, turn to steam, and expand, splitting the stone.

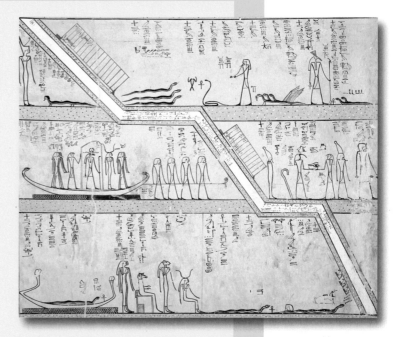

tunnel, but when it was completed, trains could pass under the river.

Once people perfected the tunnelling shield, tunnel-building technology took off. Today, machines that bore (dig) tunnels are enormous, and they can dig out tunnels at a rate of 500 feet (152 meters) per day.

The Channel Tunnel, or "Chunnel," is a railway tunnel that runs between the United Kingdom and France, under the waters of the English Channel.

Opened in 1994, the tunnel allows **freight** and passenger trains to make the 31-mile (50-kilometer) trip in a matter of minutes.

Tunnels provide trains with convenient routes past natural and artificial obstacles.

▶ The Flush Toilet

These ancient Roman toilets served the people of Ostia, Italy.

Getting rid of human waste has been a key problem for **civilizations** through the ages. In fact, the **flush toilet** has been a common feature of buildings for only about 150 years.

As far back as 2500 B.C. in the areas that are now Pakistan and western India, people built drains to remove waste from their homes. Just 500 years later, ancient people on the island of Crete built a palace that had pipes for drinking water and holes that served as toilets. Greek architects also developed a system of air **shafts** that helped clear the smells of the waste.

Ancient **Romans** created both working faucets and **sewerage** systems (system of drains) that carried waste away from homes and dumped it into nearby rivers and streams. However, the focus on waste removal stopped with the ancient Romans. From about A.D. 400 through the 1400's, waste removal systems essentially disappeared. People got rid of waste by simply throwing it into the street.

Versions of the flush toilet appeared in some ancient civilizations, but it not was further developed until the early 1500's in England. However, the lack of plumbing and sewerage systems meant that flush toilets were not yet practical.

In 1779, an Englishman named Joseph Bramah improved the design for the flush toilet. This kind of toilet was more widely adopted, but the plumbing systems that supported it had some key problems. In particular, the toilets drained into pits called

Thomas Crapper's company created this modern-style toilet in 1890.

cesspools, which could overflow and spill **sewage.** Then in the mid-1800's, people developed **septic tanks** to contain the waste.

By 1860, an English plumber named Thomas Crapper made improvements to the flush toilet. That same year, the city of London began constructing one of the first modern sewerage systems. (See Modern Sewerage Systems, pages 32-33.)

A CLOSER LOOK

During the **Middle Ages,** people in European cities simply tossed their garbage into the streets. City buildings had sidewalks in front of the main level, and the buildings' second

and third **stories** were built out over wide beams that stretched over the sidewalks. People walked below the overhangs to keep out of the way of household waste being tossed from the upper stories. However, by the late 1700's, Europeans began to realize that unsanitary living conditions were connected to disease. Cities soon established waste removal systems to collect trash from streets and waterways.

Modern Sewerage Systems

Today, cities and towns have plumbing systems that keep clean water and wastewater separate. But for much of human history, people did not understand the importance of cleaning and removing waste. Though some early **civilizations** created drainage systems to carry away waters from floods or storms, modern **sewerage** systems did not develop until the mid-1800's.

Today, buildings have a separate set of pipes to bring clean water into the building and to remove wastewater from it.

By the **Middle Ages,** European cities had terrible water problems. **Sewage** mixed with drinking water, and thousands of people died every year from diseases that were transmitted through dirty water. In London, the River Thames essentially became an open pit of sewage.

As people started to realize the connection between waste and illness, they began working to keep clean water and dirty water apart. By the 1800's, Europeans started devising ways to clean wastewater. Government officials in London had heard about the sewerage systems developed by ancient people on the island of Crete. They looked to these as an example from which they could develop their own sewerage system.

Household waste, mixed with water, flowed out of each house. This waste needed to go somewhere, but people were not sure exactly where. Cities worked to find storage solutions that were cleaner and safer than the open, sewage-filled pits they had used at first.

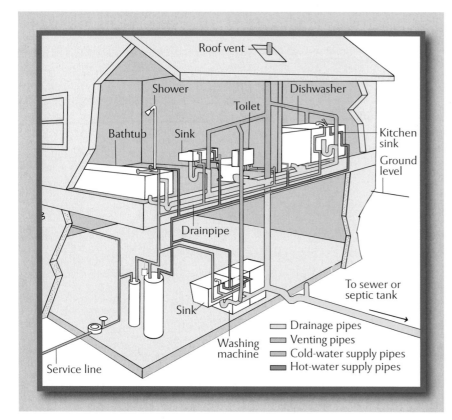

Roof vent
Shower
Dishwasher
Toilet
Bathtub
Sink
Kitchen sink
Ground level
Drainpipe
Sink
To sewer or septic tank
Washing machine
Service line

□ Drainage pipes
□ Venting pipes
□ Cold-water supply pipes
■ Hot-water supply pipes

Sewage treatment plants, like this one in Munich, Germany, are a necessity for every city.

Eventually, **engineers** and city planners made progress in their efforts to thoroughly clean wastewater. Through trial and error, they developed a **wastewater treatment system** that is now used in many parts of the world.

In such a system, sewage flows from buildings through large concrete or clay pipes that lead to a central place. There, the sewage flows into the first of a series of pools, where the cleaning process begins.

In the first stage of wastewater treatment, screens strain out large objects, such as wood, cloth, or metal. The water then rests in tanks so that large pieces of waste and dirt can settle to the bottom, forming a thick sludge. The water then moves to other tanks, where it is treated with a variety of chemicals and special filters until it is clean. It is then released into nearby waterways.

The development of modern sewerage and water treatment systems dramatically reduced the occurrences of disease. It allowed for the development of modern cities and towns as we know them today.

FUN FACT

Sewage sludge is actually full of energy. Some sewage treatment plants heat the sludge to 95 °F (35 °C). At this temperature, the sludge decomposes (breaks down) and produces methane gas. This gas can power the machinery that the sewage treatment plants use to treat the sewage.

► Central Heating

As people started to perfect the technology that brought in fresh water and carried away waste, they also looked at other ways to make their lives more pleasant and comfortable. In particular, they searched for better, more efficient ways to heat their homes.

Prehistoric hunters and gatherers built fires within their tents, making sure that a hole was open at the top of the structure to allow the smoke to flow out. When people started to settle into early farming communities, they made places in their homes for similar fires. Although the fires did help heat the homes, they also created some difficulties. The small rooms would become dark and smoky. The opening in the roof would let in rain that doused the fire or wind that blew smoke back inside. Worst of all, the fires could only heat small areas, so they were not an efficient way to heat the larger, more comfortable structures that people had learned how to build.

The ancient **Romans** figured out a system for heating some of their larger, more important buildings during the cold winters. Their system was called a **hypocaust.** With a hypocaust system, servants tended steady fires in one area of the building. The warm air from the fires then went through vents under the floors and up into the walls of other rooms.

In other areas of the world, people constructed early heating stoves. In China, as early as 100 B.C., people were using cast-iron stoves. In Europe, starting in the A.D. 1400's, people built stoves out of bricks, and later out of iron. In 1777, European inventors created heating systems that ran hot water through a series of pipes, heating the rooms above the pipes. This led to the invention of **radiators.**

In 1820, the first large **central heating** system was built in a silk factory in England. For this system, inventors figured out a way to heat water in a large boiler and then send superheated steam through cast-iron pipes and up into the rooms of the factory. By the mid-1800's, many businesses had steam heat that was pushed by fans through the ducts (pipes).

In the early 1900's, many people started constructing buildings that relied on gas heat rather than coal or wood. These systems are still in use all around the world, although the technology that runs them improves all the time. People today use **thermostats** to set the temperature they want a room to have. When the air around the thermostat cools below this temperature, the thermostat sends an **electronic** message to the heating system, triggering it to send more heat into the room.

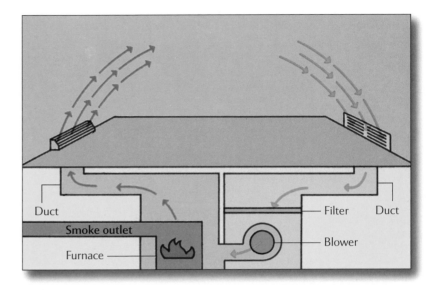

Duct

Smoke outlet

Furnace

Filter   Duct

Blower

Furnaces heat the air that is blown and circulated throughout the house.

Benjamin Franklin

Benjamin Franklin (1706-1790) was a famous printer, publisher, author, and politician. Franklin was also a talented inventor. In the early 1740's, he invented an efficient stove, which to this day is still called a Franklin stove. Built out of cast iron, it fit into a fireplace but extended forward, so that it gave off heat from its three sides. Franklin didn't stop there. He invented many common items, such as bifocal glasses, and even early harmonicas. He was also one of the first people to study and harness electricity. His experiment with a kite and key during a thunderstorm proved that lightning was electricity. This discovery led him to invent lightning rods that are still used to protect buildings all around the world.

▶ Air Conditioning

Just as people sought to heat their homes during cold winters, they also tried to keep cool during the hot summer months. These efforts led to the development of **air conditioning.**

Ancient Egyptians, Greeks, and **Romans** cooled indoor air by hanging wet mats in open doorways and windows. When the wind blew through the wet mats, the **evaporating** water cooled the air. In 1500, the Italian artist and scientist Leonardo da Vinci built the first mechanical fan, which was powered by water.

Cities, with all their concrete and **industry,** are often much warmer than the surrounding countrysides. As a result, people in cities had to work even harder to stay cool. Over time, business leaders realized that high temperatures in the workplace made it difficult for workers to stay healthy and do their jobs. As a result, the development of cooling systems became even more important.

In the mid-1800's, an American doctor named John Gorrie invented a cold-air machine. Gorrie practiced medicine in Florida, where the weather is often very hot. He used his machine to keep hospital rooms cool and comfortable. The machine, invented in 1851, made ice in the same sort of way that modern freezers do.

About 50 years later, an **engineer** named Alfred R. Wolff figured out a way to build air-cooling machines for Carnegie Hall and several other important buildings in New York City. At the same time, an engineer named Willis H. Carrier invented a machine

Cooling systems, like this one from 1887, chilled food on long sea voyages.

that could clean and circulate air and control the air's temperature and humidity (amount of water vapor).

By 1922, the first completely air-conditioned office buildings were being built. As technology improved, people started building air conditioning into trains, cars, and private homes.

Today, many people who live in hot climates use air conditioning. About 80 percent of American homes have air conditioners. In some Asian countries, the percentage is even higher.

Willis Carrier, shown standing next to his "chiller" in 1922, helped bring air conditioning to millions of people.

FUN FACT In 1906, Stuart W. Cramer, a textile engineer from North Carolina, used the term *air conditioning* for the first time. Air conditioning became a recognized branch of engineering in 1911.

Modern air conditioning systems have a thermostat that can be adjusted to control room temperature.

► Electric Elevators

Elisha Otis demonstrates his elevator brake in 1854.

As new people and businesses arrived in cities each year, space became more and more valuable. To find enough land to support growth, cities spread outward into nearby countrysides. When cities could not spread out into new lands, architects took a different approach: They built up.

Before the late 1800's, buildings were usually only a couple of **stories** tall. But as growing cities needed more and more space, architects started making taller buildings. Of course, the tall buildings had long staircases, and it often took great effort for people to climb to the upper floors. The climb became even more difficult when people had to carry heavy furniture or business supplies.

Inventors addressed this problem by developing elevators. To make sure that the elevators worked safely and steadily, they built the elevators into thin **shafts** that were as tall as the building. The elevator would then move up and down guide rails in the shaft, so that it would not swing sideways on the ropes that suspended it.

The earliest elevators were powered with water power or steam power. These elevators were slow and dangerous. The ropes that hauled the steam-powered elevators often broke, sending the elevator cars crashing to the bottom of the shaft.

In the 1850's, a New Yorker named Elisha Graves Otis invented a safety device that kept elevators from falling, even if the ropes broke.

To prove the safety of his invention, Otis rode up to the top of a building and then had the rope cut to prove that the elevator would not fall.

Production of passenger elevators started in 1857. In 1880, a German inventor named Ernst Werner von Siemens (*SEE muhnz* or *ZEE muhnz*) introduced the first **electric elevator.** Electric elevators were safe and reliable. Never before could people travel up a building so quickly and easily.

The invention of the electric elevator made it possible for people to build taller and taller buildings. It is no wonder that the first skyscrapers began to emerge around this time.

Electric elevators, like this one in Southampton, England, take people quickly up and down tall buildings.

F U N F A C T People were thinking about building elevators long before there were tall buildings that needed them. As far back as 230 B.C., a Greek mathematician named Archimedes (*AHR kuh MEE deez*) designed an elevator using ropes and pulleys. It could lift one person—a great idea to start with, but it wasn't quite ready for use in a modern skyscraper!

▶ Skyscrapers

By the late 1800's, architects were trying to turn thousands of years of construction knowledge into a solution for crowded cities. Huge numbers of people wanted their homes and businesses located in the centers of cities, and city planners tried to meet people's needs by making taller buildings. The more **stories** a building has, the more homes and businesses it can hold.

As architects looked to create the first **skyscrapers,** they made use of past breakthroughs in building. The invention of **electric elevators** solved one big problem—how to get people and materials to the upper floors. Improved building techniques and strong, durable materials also made the job easier.

Steel construction beams opened up a completely new world in architecture. For thousands of years, people had considered stone to be the strongest building material. However, stone buildings, because of their great weight, tended to collapse on themselves if they were built too high. With the steel beams, it seemed there was no limit to how high new buildings could be.

Architects and **engineers** soon learned how to build steel frameworks for tall buildings. These frameworks act as kind of a skeleton around which the building is constructed. The new buildings also had

Steel frameworks made the building of skyscrapers possible.

deep **foundations** that could go hundreds of feet below the ground into solid rock. The steel skeleton balanced on concrete or steel **columns** in the foundation, which spread the load of the building over the solid rock in the earth.

Architects who built skyscrapers faced new challenges, such as how to construct buildings that could withstand strong winds or earthquakes. As they improved their designs and strengthened their structures, the buildings continued to grow.

The world's first skyscrapers were built in Chicago and New York City. Today, almost every major city in the world has skyscrapers. Some of the most famous include the Shanghai World Financial Center in Shanghai, China; the Sears Tower in Chicago; and the Empire State Building in New York City.

The Taipei 101 building in Taiwan is one of the tallest skyscrapers in the world.

FUN FACT When designing skyscrapers, architects consider the natural elements the building may face. For example, architects of the First Interstate World Center in Los Angeles, California, had to construct the building so it would be stiff enough to stand against the wind and storms that blow in from the ocean. They also had to make its foundation flexible enough to withstand earthquakes. Today, the skyscraper is one of the tallest buildings in the United States.

▶ Solar Energy

Over thousands of years, architects and city planners have tackled every challenge on their way to building bigger and stronger buildings. However, along with these advances, new sets of challenges have emerged.

The huge buildings and complex cities of today require a great deal of energy for heating and electric power. Most of this energy comes from **fossil fuels** (coal, oil, or natural gas). This reliance on fossil fuels presents problems. First, Earth has only a limited amount of fossil fuels, and eventually the supply will run out. In addition, the burning of fossil fuels creates a great deal of **pollution.** This pollution poisons the environment. It also contributes to **global warming.**

As people have become more aware of the problems associated with fossil fuels, they have looked for alternative ways to provide energy. One alternative involves **solar energy**—that is, the energy that comes from sunlight.

The basic idea of solar-powered buildings dates back to the earliest architects, whose structures relied on sunlight for heat and light. Modern solar homes combine this basic idea

Solar panels contain small devices that convert the sun's energy into electric power.

The Native Americans of Mesa Verde, Colorado, built their homes to collect sunlight and heat in winter and to provide shade and cooler air in summer.

with technologies that can turn the sun's rays into the energy needed to power the home.

In 1839, a French scientist named Alexandre Edmond Becquerel first discovered that solar energy could be stored in cells and converted into electric power. However, it would take more than 100 years for scientists to develop a solar cell that could produce a useful amount of power.

In the 1970's, the American **engineer** James Tennant Baldwin helped develop the first modern building ever to be powered completely by solar and wind energy.

Today, people can install **solar panels** on a building's rooftop to supply energy for their home. These panels contain a group of small devices that collect the sun's heat as energy and convert it into electric power.

Solar energy can also be used to heat buildings. The sunlight is collected and used to heat air or water, which then circulates throughout the building.

Presently, solar energy is often a more expensive power source than fossil fuels. However, solar technology is improving rapidly. Scientists and architects hope that solar energy will someday provide a clean and reliable source of power for most modern buildings.

FUN FACT
Every hour, enough sunlight falls on Earth to meet the world's demand for power for one year.

c. 2800 B.C. Egyptians built the earliest known dam.

c. 2600's B.C. The most famous Egyptian pyramids were built in Giza.

c. 2500 B.C. The earliest arches were built.

c. 2500 B.C. People in southern Asia built drains to remove waste from their homes.

c. 2000 B.C. People on the island of Crete built a palace that had water pipes and holes that served as toilets.

c. 230 B.C. Archimedes designed a basic elevator.

33 B.C. Marcus Agrippa, who ordered the construction of many aqueducts, became Rome's water commissioner.

A.D. 126 The Pantheon was completed in ancient Rome.

A.D. 500's One of the oldest standing pagodas, the Pagoda of Chongyuesi Temple, was built.

1436 The dome of the Cathedral of Florence was completed.

1500 Leonardo da Vinci built the first mechanical fan.

Early 1500's The first flushing toilet was created.

1500's The use of trusses led to more sophisticated bridge designs.

1590 The dome atop St. Peter's

LEONARDO DA VINCI

Basilica in Vatican City was completed.

1777 European inventors created heating systems that led to the invention of radiators.

1779 Joseph Bramah figured out an improved design for a flushing toilet.

Early 1800's People began constructing massive suspension bridges.

1800's Europeans started developing ways to clean wastewater.

1820 The first large central heating system was built in an English factory.

1851 John Gorrie invented a cold-air machine.

1880 Ernst Werner von Siemens introduced the first electric elevator.

1880's The world's first skyscrapers rose in Chicago and New York City.

1906 Stuart W. Cramer first used the term *air conditioning*.

1920's The first completely air-conditioned office buildings were built.

1937 The Golden Gate Bridge in San Francisco was completed.

1970's James Tennant Baldwin helped develop the first modern building ever to be powered completely by solar energy.

1994 The Channel Tunnel opened, allowing for railway travel between the United Kingdom and France.

Glossary

air conditioning a system for controlling the temperature, moisture, cleanliness, and movement of indoor air.

aqueduct an artificial channel through which water is conducted to the place where it is used.

arcade a series of arches supported by columns or piers. A passageway formed by the arches is also called an arcade.

arch a curved structure used to support the weight of the material above it.

Buddhist relating to Buddhism, a religion that developed in the 500's B.C., in northern India and spread over central, southeastern, and eastern Asia.

canal a waterway dug across land.

cantilever a horizontal projection, such as a balcony or a beam, that is supported only at one end.

central heating the heating of one building or a group of buildings from a single source.

civilization nations and peoples that have reached advanced stages in social development.

column a vertical support.

dam a barrier placed across a river to stop the flow of water.

dome a curved roof, much like a bowl turned upside down.

drawbridge a bridge that can be entirely or partly lifted, lowered, or moved to one side.

drought a long period of dry weather.

electric elevator a lifting device, powered by an electric system, that carries people and freight to the floors of a building.

electronic of or having to do with electrons, which are negatively charged particles in atoms.

engineer; engineering a person who plans and builds engines, machines, roads, bridges, canals, forts, or the like; the use of science to design structures, machines, and products.

evaporate to change from a liquid or solid into a vapor (gas).

flush toilet a toilet that gets rid of human waste by using water to flush it through a pipe into another location.

foundation the base on which the other parts of a building or structure rest for support.

fortress a place built with walls and defenses.

fossil fuels natural fuels, such as coal, oil, and natural gas. These fuels are obtained from underground deposits that were formed millions of years ago from the remains of plants and animals.

freight goods that a train, truck, ship, or aircraft carries.

girder a main supporting beam, made of steel, concrete, or wood.

global warming an increase in the average temperature at Earth's surface.

grid an arrangement of intersecting vertical and horizontal lines.

hypocaust a system for heating a building by circulating warm air from a special fire room.

industry any branch of business, trade, or manufacture.

keystone the middle stone at the top of an arch.

Mesopotamia an ancient region in the Middle East in which the world's earliest civilization developed.

Middle Ages the period in European history between ancient and modern times, from about the A.D. 400's through the 1400's.

mine a large hole or space dug in the earth to get out ores, precious stones, coal, salt, or anything valuable.

moat a deep, wide ditch dug around a castle or town as a protection against enemies.

Muslim relating to Islam, the name given to the religion preached by the Prophet Muhammad in the A.D. 600's.

overcrowding the problem of having more people than an area's land and resources can support.

pagoda a type of tower commonly associated with Buddhist temples.

pier a support on which a bridge rests. The term may also refer to any solid support, especially of masonry, that bears pressure from above.

polluted; pollution filled with harmful wastes; harm to the natural environment caused by human activity. Pollution dirties the land, air, or water.

pyramid a large structure with four triangular sides that come to a point at the top.

radiator a set of pipes or tubes that gives off heat to its surroundings.

Renaissance a great cultural movement that began in Italy during the early 1300's.

reservoir a place where large quantities of water are stored.

Roman of or having to do with ancient Rome or its people. The Roman Empire controlled most of Europe and the Middle East from 27 B.C. to A.D. 476.

septic tank a tank in which sewage is broken down.

sewage water that contains waste matter produced by human beings.

sewerage the removal of waste matter by sewers.

shaft a long, narrow passage.

skyscraper an extremely tall building.

solar energy the direct use of sunlight to produce heat or electric power.

solar panel a panel of small devices that convert the energy in sunlight into electric power.

Stone Age the earliest known period of human culture, in which people used tools and weapons made from stone.

story the level of a building above ground.

stupa a dome-shaped monumental structure usually found in Buddhist countries.

suspension bridge a bridge that has a roadway hanging from steel cables that are supported by two high towers.

thermostat a device that helps control the temperature of an indoor area or of an appliance.

truss a framework of beams or other supports usually connected in a series of triangles and used to form a support for a roof or bridge.

tunnelling shield a steel cylinder that holds up the roof and walls of a tunnel.

turret a small tower, often on the corner of a building.

wastewater treatment system a system of removing wastewater from buildings and cleaning it through a series of stages.

▶ Additional Resources

Books:

- *Amazing Leonardo da Vinci Inventions You Can Build Yourself* by Maxine Anderson (Nomad Press VT, 2006).

- *Building Big* by David Macaulay (Houghton Mifflin, 2000).

- *Gargoyles, Girders, and Glass Houses* by Bo Zaunders (Dutton, 2004).

- *Great Inventions : The Illustrated Science Encyclopedia* by Peter Harrison, Chris Oxlade, and Stephen Bennington (Southwater Publishing, 2001).

- *Great Inventions of the 20th Century* by Peter Jedicke (Chelsea House Publications, 2007).

- *Inventions* by Valerie Wyatt (Kids Can Press, 2003).

- *Skyscrapers* by Chris Oxlade (Heinemann Library, 2006).

- *So You Want to Be an Inventor?* By Judith St. George (Philomel Books, 2002).

- *What a Great Idea! Inventions that Changed the World* by Stephen M. Tomecek (Scholastic, 2003).

Web Sites:

- Ancient Greece
  http://www.ancientgreece.com/s/Art
  Explore the history of art and architecture in the ancient Greek world.

- History for Kids: Ancient and Medieval Architecture
  http://www.historyforkids.org/learn/architecture
  Find out more about the history of ancient and medieval architecture on this student-friendly Web site.

- Byzantine Architecture Project
  http://www.princeton.edu/~asce/const_95/const.html
  This Web site includes information about a project at Princeton University to study architecture from the Byzantine Empire.

- The Great Buildings Collection
  http://www.greatbuildings.com
  Architecture Week's Great Buildings Web site features illustrations of more than 1000 buildings from around the world.

- National Building Museum
  http://www.nbm.org/families-kids
  Information for students from the National Building Museum in Washington, D.C.

- National Inventors Hall of Fame
  http://www.invent.org/index.asp
  Information on inventions and inventors from the National Inventors Hall of Fame.

- Skyscraper Page
  http://skyscraperpage.com
  Information on skyscrapers from around the world.

▶ Index